You're One Fine Chick!

Paintings by Deb Strain

HARVEST HOUSE PUBLISHERS
EUGENE, OREGON

You're One Fine Chick

Text Copyright © 2005 by Harvest House Publishers
Eugene, Oregon 97402

ISBN-13: 978-0-7369-1491-8
ISBN-10: 0-7369-1491-9

Artwork © Deb Strain by arrangement with Mosaic Licensing. It may not be copied or reproduced without permission. For more information regarding artwork featured in this book, please contact:

> Mosaic Licensing
> 675 Ygnacio Valley Road, Suite B207
> Walnut Creek, CA 94596
> (925) 934-0889

Design and production by Garborg Design Works, Minneapolis, Minnesota

Harvest House Publishers has made every effort to trace the ownership of all poems and quotes. In the event of a question arising from the use of a poem or quote, we regret any error made and will be pleased to make the necessary correction in future editions of this book.

Scripture quotations are taken from the Holy Bible, New International Version®, Copyright © 1973, 1978, 1984 by the International Bible Society. Used by permission of Zondervan. All rights reserved.

Printed in China

06 07 08 09 10 11 12 / IM / 10 9 8 7 6 5 4 3

To My Friend,

Joann

With Love,

Galeen

You're one
fine chick!

*You just reminded me of what's really
important in life—friends, best friends.*

FANNIE FLAGG

And the pleasantness of one's friend springs from his earnest counsel.

THE BOOK OF PROVERBS

Let's become little old ladies together—we'll stay up late looking at old
pictures, telling "remember when" stories, and laughing till our sides ache.
Let's become eccentric together—the kind of old ladies who take long walks,
wear silly hats, and get away with acting outrageous in public places.
And if anybody should ask how long we've been friends, we'll say,
"Oh, forever—since before you were even born!"
Let's become little old ladies together—because a friendship that's
as special as ours can only grow better through the years.

AUTHOR UNKNOWN

And when you are comforted (time soothes all sorrows) you will be happy to have known me. You will always be my friend.

ANTOINE DE SAINT-EXUPÉRY

We started being "we" before we were born…We are everything to one another. We don't need to say so; it's just true. Sometimes it seems like we're so close we form one single complete person…You know what the secret is? It's so simple. We love one another. We're nice to one another. Do you know how rare that is?

ANN BRASHARES
Sisterhood of the Traveling Pants

Few delights can equal the mere presence of one whom we utterly trust.

GEORGE MACDONALD

© Deb Strain

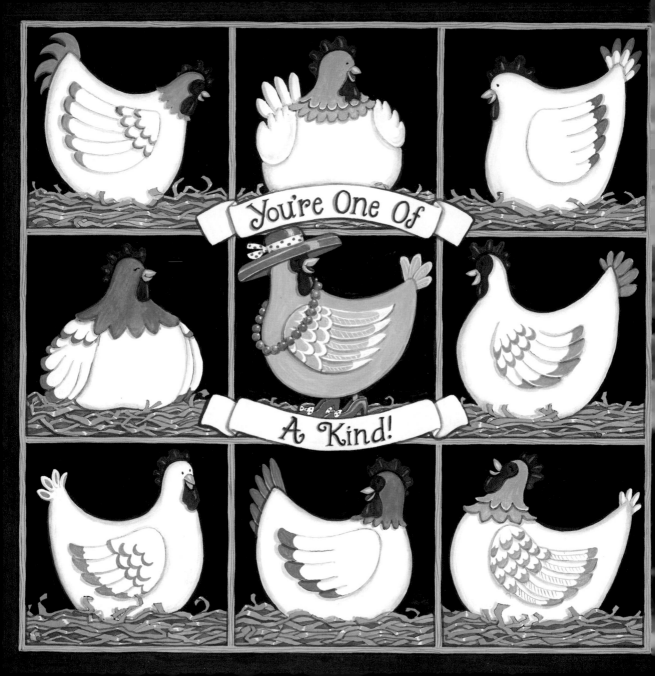

Piglet sidled up to Pooh.
"Pooh!" he whispered.
"Yes, Piglet?"
"Nothing," said Piglet, taking Pooh's paw.
"I just wanted to be sure of you."

A.A. MILNE

Madam, I have been looking for a person who disliked gravy all my life; let us swear eternal friendship.

SYDNEY SMITH

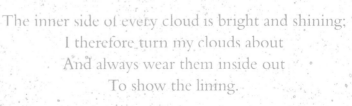

The inner side of every cloud is bright and shining;
I therefore turn my clouds about
And always wear them inside out
To show the lining.

ELLEN THORNCROFT FOWLER

9

O the world is wide and the world is grand,
And there's little or nothing new,
But its sweetest thing is the grip of the hand
Of the friend who's tried and true.

Of all the means to insure happiness
throughout the whole life, by far the most
important is the acquisition of friends.

11

Friendship is a serious affection; the most sublime of all affections, because it is founded on principle and cemented by time.

AUTHOR UNKNOWN

There are persons so radiant,
so genial, so kind,
so pleasure-bearing, that you
instinctively feel in
their presence that they do
you good, whose coming
into a room is like the
bringing of a lamp there.

HENRY WARD BEECHER

A friend loves at all times.

THE BOOK OF PROVERBS

Viz'tin. That's what the Ya-Yas called their impromptu get togethers when Sidda was a girl. The four Walker kids crammed into the T-Bird with Vivi, bombing into town to Caro's or Teensy's or Necie's, pulling into the driveway, madly blowing the horn, shouting out, "Ya'll *better* be home!" Then beverages appeared, and cream cheese with Pickapeppa and crackers, a gallon of lemonade and Oreos for the kids, Sarah Vaughan on the stereo, and a party. No planning. No calls in advance.

REBECCA WELLS
Divine Secrets of the Ya-Ya Sisterhood

Happy is the house that shelters a friend.

RALPH WALDO EMERSON

A friendship can weather most things and thrive in thin soil, but it needs just a little mulch of letters and phone calls and small, silly presents every so often—just to save it from drying out completely.

PAM BROWN

It is only with the heart that one can see rightly; what is essential is invisible to the eye.

ANTOINE DE SAINT-EXUPERY

We are sometimes made aware of a kindness long passed, and realize that there have been times when our friends' thoughts of us were of so pure and lofty a character that they passed over us like the winds of heaven unnoticed; when they treat us not as what we were, but as what we aspired to be.

HENRY DAVID THOREAU

You're such a nice person,
No matter the season,
That you're in my thoughts
Without any reason.
You're friendly and cheerful
Each day of the year,
And folks always smile
Whenever you're near.
During the day
I quite often find
A kind word or deed
Brings you to my mind.
You're such a nice person
And I'd like to say
That just thinking of you
Brings pleasure my way!

PATRICIA MANGEAU

©Deb Strain

Every day we live is a priceless gift of God,
loaded with possibilities to learn something new,
to gain fresh insights into His great truths.

DALE EVANS ROGERS

Friendship only is, indeed, genuine when two friends, without speaking a word to each other, can nevertheless find happiness in being together.

GEORGE EBERS

I believe laughter is like a needle and thread.
Deftly used, it can patch up just about everything.

BARBARA JOHNSON

Happiness comes of the capacity to feel deeply, to enjoy simply, to think freely, to risk life, to be needed.

STORM JAMESON

A true friend unbosoms freely,
advises justly, assists readily,
adventures boldly, takes all patiently,
defends courageously, and continues
a friend unchangeably.

WILLIAM PENN

Knit your hearts with an unslipping knot.

WILLIAM SHAKESPEARE

The more one does and sees and feels,
the more one is able to do, and the
more genuine may be one's appreciation
of fundamental things like home, and
love, and understanding companionship.

AMELIA EARHART

I have not stopped giving thanks for you, remembering you in my prayers.

THE BOOK OF EPHESIANS

In pleasure's dream, or sorrow's hour,
In crowded hall or lonely bower,
The business of my soul shall be
Forever to remember thee!

BENJAMIN FRANKLIN

A gentle heart is tied with an easy thread.

GEORGE HERBERT

© Deb Strain

© Deb Strain

The side porch—that's where the Ya-Yas went if their hair was in pin curls, when they didn't want to wave and chat to passersby. This is where they sighed, this is where they dreamed. This is where they lay for hours, contemplating their navels, sweating, dozing, swatting flies, trading secrets there on the porch in a hot, humid girl soup. And in the evening when the sun went down and the fireflies would light up over by the camellias, and that little nimbus of light would lull the Ya-Yas even deeper into porch reveries. Reveries that would linger even as they aged.

REBECCA WELLS
Divine Secrets of the Ya-Ya Sisterhood

All the beautiful sentiments in the world weigh less than a single lovely action.

JAMES RUSSELL LOWELL

Some people think only intellect counts: knowing how to solve problems, knowing how to get by, knowing how to identify an advantage and seize it. But the functions of intellect are insufficient without courage, love, friendship, compassion and empathy.

DEAN KOONTZ

The best mirror is an old friend.

GEORGE HERBERT

*Never look back...
Never regret...
Never remember
the people you've met.
Never begin...
And never end...
Never say never when it comes to your friends!*

ALIZA LLAGUNO

29

Carole and Stevie heaved a joint sigh of relief and sat down on either side of Lisa to give her a big three-way hug...She had taken a big, difficult first step, and they were going to stick with her every step of the way. That was what friends were for.

BONNIE BRYANT
Summer Rider

What sunshine is to flowers, smiles are to humanity. They are but trifles, to be sure but, scattered along life's pathway, the good they do is inconceivable.

AUTHOR UNKNOWN

True friendship is like sound health;
the value of it is seldom known until it be lost.

CHARLES CALEB COLTON

Treat people as if they were what they ought to be and you help them to become what they are capable of being.

GOETHE

It's the friends you can call up at 4 AM that matter.

MARLENE DIETRICH

The most beautiful discovery that true friends can make is that they can grow separately without growing apart.

ELIZABETH FOLEY

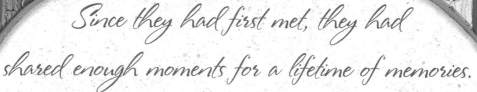

Since they had first met, they had shared enough moments for a lifetime of memories.

VIRGINIA DeBERRY & DONNA GRANT
Better Than I Know Myself

I feel I am more blessed than many people because I have this kind of a friend in my life. A friend who is always there for me no matter what. A friend who accepts me as I am but loves me too much to let me stay that way. Yes, I would say I am blessed because I have a true friend.

ROBIN JONES GUNN
True Friends

Friendship is always a sweet responsibility, never an opportunity.

KAHLIL GIBRAN

© Deb Strain

A real friend will tell you when you have spinach stuck in your teeth.

AUTHOR UNKNOWN

Friendship that flows from the heart cannot be frozen by adversity, as the water that flows from the spring cannot congeal in winter.

JAMES FENIMORE COOPER

A reassuring presence,
A light when times are dark,
A hand reaching out,
Is what friendship is about.

AUTHOR UNKNOWN

Every gift from a friend is a wish for your happiness...

RICHARD BACH

37

Those who bring sunshine into the lives of others cannot help but keep it from themselves.

SIR JAMES BARRIE

Friendship is like a Christmas tree, decorated with warm memories and shared joys. You're the slightly cracked ornament that always makes me smile.

AUTHOR UNKNOWN

Ships on the ocean, ships on the sea, but the best ship is the friendship between you and me.

AUTHOR UNKNOWN

© Deb Strain

When we honestly ask ourselves which person in our lives means the most to us, we often find that it is those who, instead of giving advice, solutions, or cures, have chosen rather to share our pain and touch our wounds with a warm and tender hand. The friend who can be silent with us in a moment of despair or confusion, who can stay with us in an hour of grief and bereavement, who can tolerate not knowing, not curing, not healing and face with us the reality of our powerlessness, that is a friend who cares.

HENRI NOUWEN

Friendship isn't a big thing—it's a million little things.

AUTHOR UNKNOWN

In the sweetness of friendship let there be laughter, for in the dew of little things the heart finds its morning and is refreshed.

JAMES ALLEN

Beginnings are always scary, endings are usually sad, but it's the middle that counts. You just have to give hope a chance to float up.

STEVEN ROGERS

But if the while I think on thee, dear friend, All losses are restored and sorrows end.

WILLIAM SHAKESPEARE

Savor the moments that are warm and special and giggly.

SAMMY DAVIS JR.

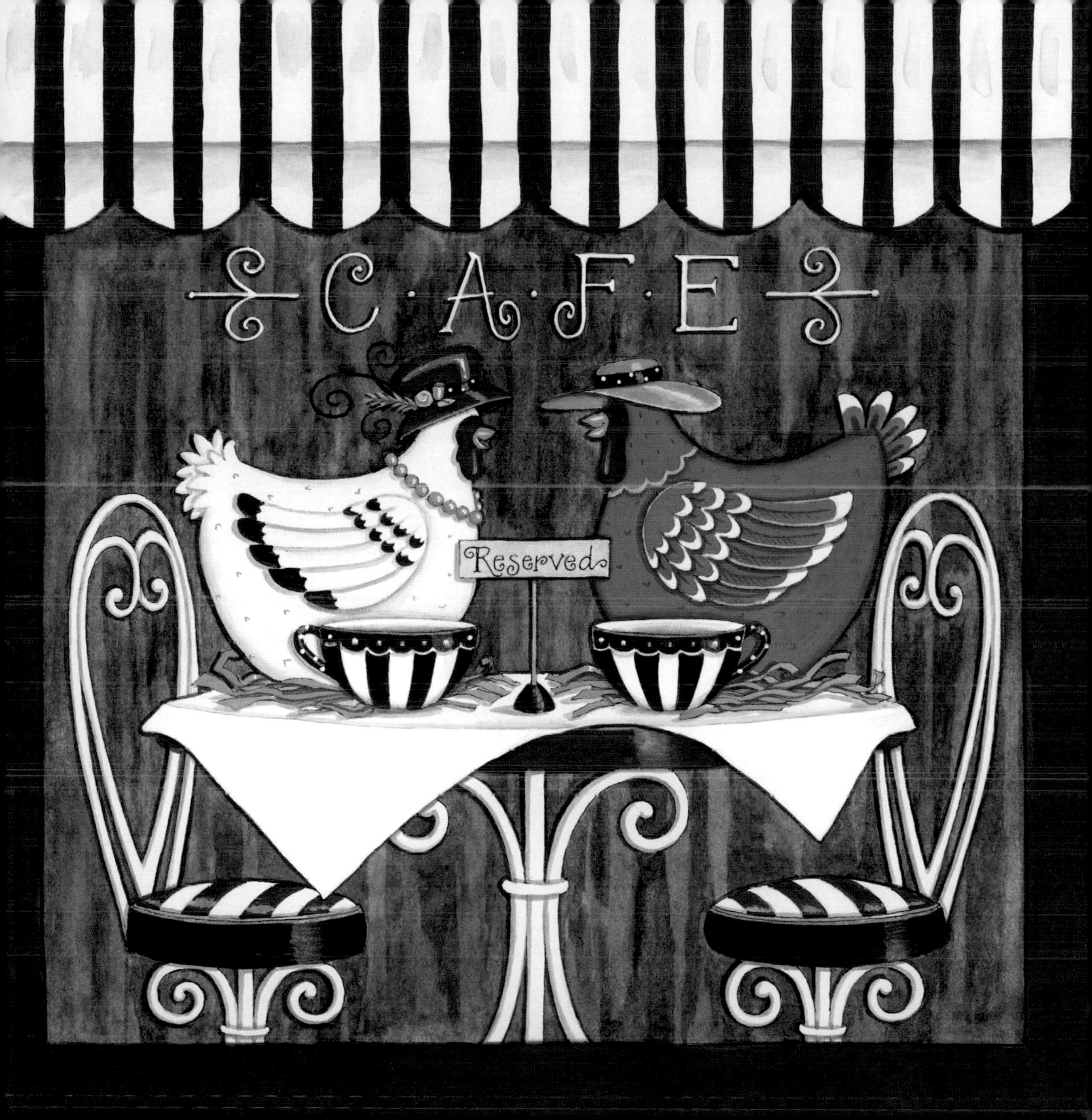
CAFE
Reserved

If you're alone, I'll be your shadow. If you want to cry, I'll be your shoulder. If you want a hug, I'll be your pillow. If you need to be happy, I'll be your smile. But anytime you need a friend, I'll just be me.

AUTHOR UNKNOWN

You're One Of A Kind!

She is a friend of mind.
She gather me, man.
The pieces I am, she gather
them and give them back
to me in all the right order.
It's good, you know, when
you got a woman who
is a friend of your mind.

TONI MORRISON
Beloved

Constant use will not wear ragged the fabric of friendship.

DOROTHY PARKER

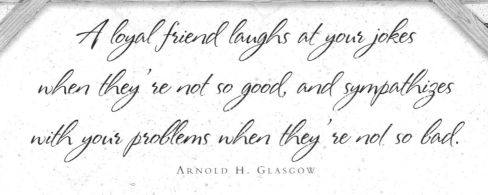

A loyal friend laughs at your jokes when they're not so good, and sympathizes with your problems when they're not so bad.

ARNOLD H. GLASGOW

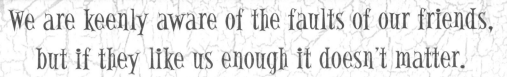

We are keenly aware of the faults of our friends, but if they like us enough it doesn't matter.

MIGNON MCLAUGHLIN

I have friends in overalls whose friendship I would not swap for the favor of the kings of the world.

THOMAS A. EDISON

The five of them ran headlong into the lake and began dragging out a large piece of driftwood. Working together, they pulled the log onto the beach and balanced it on a large rock. This took quite some time, and as she watched, they gave each other directions and encouragement. When the piece of wood was finally on the rock, the girls stood back and admired their work.

"A seesaw!" the girl with the pigtails called out.

"A seesaw by the seashore!" one of the other girls said.

REBECCA WELLS
Divine Secrets of the Ya-Ya Sisterhood